The Psychology of Aging and Loneliness

Dr. Asghar Mojtahedzadeh

Copyright © 2019 Asghar Mojtahedzadeh
All rights reserved. No part of this book may be reprinted or reproduced utilized in any form or by any electronic, mechanical, or other means now known or hereafter invented, including photocopying and recording, or in any information storage or retrieval system, without permission in writing from the author;
asghar.mojtahedzadeh@yahoo.com.au

Title: The Psychology of Aging and Loneliness
Author: Dr.Asghar Mojtahedzadeh
Cover Design: Mohsen Rahmandoust
ISBN-10: 1-947464-11-6
ISBN-13: 978-1-947464-11-7
Published by American Academic Research, Reseda, CA
Printed in the United State of America

DEDICATION

I would like to dedicate this book to my mother who is very dear to me.

ACKNOWLEDGMENTS

I would like to thank Dr. Emad Khayati for his contribution as well as Dr. Farhadi and all the dear ones in the ASAN NASHR for their Excellency..

CONTENTS

Contents

Preface 1
Introduction 2
Elderly Definition 9
Features of aging 11
Elderly feelings 12
Psychological Changes in Elderly 14
Elderly and family relationship 18
Adaptation to Elderly 21
    What do the elderly need? 23
    Social support for the elderly 23
The Role of Continuing Education in Elderly Mental Health 25
Depression in the elderly 28
    Lonely in the elderly 33
    Disability in self-care: 38
    Physical conditions 39
Recommendations for Mental Health 43
Danger Symptoms 46
conclusion 55
REFERENCES 56

Preface

The phenomenon of aging is a natural path. Elderly is actually the biological changes that appear in a person's bio-organism and psychosocial status over time. These changes, by reducing the adaptive force of the individual, reduce the ability to adapt to sudden changes and the inability to rebalance and gradually bring about changes in the structure and practice of the different organs of the individual (and generally refer to people over 65). The present book seeks to examine the psychological and emotional consequences of the elderly.

Introduction

Nowadays, the phenomenon of aging in all its psychological, social, cultural, religious and economic dimensions, including serious and challenging issues for families in particular and for society in general, has been developed and developed in developing countries. The phenomenon of degradation of the status of society in society has begun since the beginning of the European Industrial Revolution and has gradually expanded to other societies, with the result that the aging of human society and the values of human society have been crumbling under the rug of industrial society, and to this day, every moment witnesses the gap. Significant Fault Between Honor, Dignity, Honor, and Sacrifice for the Elderly and the Family and Human Community Environment A number of factors have led to a gap between generations and the emotional divide between generations and the overwhelming need to serve the elderly in different societies. The product of this industrialization is the proliferation of machine thinking and life in the nuclear format. We find that in most societies of families who have called for mechanical machinery, their parents are headed to loneliness and separation (the elderly) on the eve of old age, and this raises a great deal of adverse psychological and emotional consequences for the elderly, This is followed by approximately 40 % of the total number of psychiatric hospitalizations in the elderly. Elderly can be studied from four points of view: temporal, psycho-biological, psycho-emotional and social (the simplest way to define age is to count the number of years since birth).

The phenomenon of population growth is one of the most important economic, social and health challenges of the 21st century. Elderly due to the aging process, multiple problems such as chronic illnesses, psychological disorders, mild to severe dementia and depression, need to be hospitalized repeatedly, reduced life expectancy, a series of absences including loss of spouse and partner, The economic situation is experiencing a decline in physical health and in general a loss of independence and individual dependency.

Depression is a common mental disorder characterized by depressed mood, loss of motivation, lack of physical energy, inability to enjoy pleasure, sleep disturbance, feelings of hopelessness, disability and worthlessness, and ultimately a loss of focus. Depression is one of the most common mental health problems in the elderly, which is prevalent in different parts of the world and can be manifested in mild, bipolar disorder and Dysthymia disorder. The cause of depression in older people, like younger people, is the social-biological cause. Diseases and physical disorders are some of the drugs that are effective in depression. Age is an independent and important variable that can influence the onset of depression, its symptoms and its natural course. Depression is typically a major cause of mortality worldwide, which is associated with a decrease in social, occupational, and interpersonal roles.

Worse, this dreadful mental condition is often exacerbated by environmental and physical factors as we age. Numerous studies have reported estimates of the prevalence of depression in different elderly populations. The prevalence of depression and loneliness in the elderly in the whole country was 4.22%. In another study, the prevalence of depression was reported as mild depression at 8.16% and major depression at 7.14%. The National Institutes of Health for Major Depression occurs in 1 to 3 percent of the elderly population. And in addition, 16 to 8 percent of them have clinical symptoms of depression. According to Biles, depression often occurs in 12 to 16 percent of older people, though 20 to 30 percent sometimes show symptoms of depression. In addition, the study of depressed adults shows that people with depressive symptoms, people with depression or those with no depressive disorder have poorer performance, equal to or worse than people with chronic medical conditions, such as heart disease, Arthritis, hypertension and diabetes. In addition to depression, poor perception of health increases poor use of health services and costs of health services. Despite the relatively high prevalence of depression in middle-aged and elderly patients, it is often not properly diagnosed, which may be due to the belief that depressed mood is a natural consequence of aging.

According to one study, only about 10% of older people Treating Depression Even among those diagnosed and treated, the effectiveness of interventions seems relatively low.

As the elderly population increases, the community will face serious problems and problems, so the elderly and the special conditions of the elderly and their mental health are among the issues that require special attention. Appropriate intervention to prevent depression among the elderly population, risk factors for depression in this population should be identified. The aim of this study was to determine the risk factors for depression among the elderly population through systematic review of preliminary research in this field.

Given the increasing growth of the elderly, attention to their quality of life is one of the key factors in social health. Feeling lonely is one of the factors affecting the quality of life of the elderly. Therefore, the purpose of this study was to describe and explain older people's experiences of loneliness. Findings from older women's experiences of loneliness in 5 main themes including "causes of elderly feeling lonely", "physical conditions", "abuse", "positive attitude to the elderly" And "ways to reduce loneliness" were identified, and sub-themes included avoiding activities of interest, marrying and separating children and the death of a spouse, hearing problems, leg pain, Alzheimer's, being overweight, family rejection, disrupting children's lives. , Blessings of home, conscientiousness, attachment to children, increased relationship with God and attendance at religious sites, attention to physical health The elderly and increased social relations elderly out of the main themes is obtained. Developing supportive strategies by family members, health care providers, and policymakers, and adopting programs to educate families on the need for elderly families by governments in the health system are essential.

Aging is a critical period of human life and attention to the issues and needs of this stage is a social necessity. The population growth of the elderly is so significant that it is referred to as the silent revolution. Examination of statistical indices shows growth and acceleration of aging. The world's aging population is growing rapidly today. According to the UN Population Division projections, the proportion of the world's elderly population will increase by about 22% per year. Elderly people have more physical, social, and economic problems than other age groups due to a decrease in physical strength. Experiencing some anxiety about natural death. But if this anxiety is too severe, it weakens effective adaptation. Anxiety of death is defined as an abnormally high fear of death with a feeling of fear of death or fear when thinking about the process of dying or the things that happen after death. The level of death anxiety in individuals can vary due to individual differences and many social factors. Because anxiety is a multidimensional death-defying instrument, it can be expected to affect many aspects of older people's lives. Mindfulness is one of the factors that can affect people's anxiety. Mindfulness is characterized by moment-by-moment, continuous, and non-evaluative awareness of psychological processes and includes constant awareness of physical emotions, perceptions, emotions, thoughts, and perceptions. The consciousness of consciousness consists of a receptive consciousness free from judgment of current events. Elderly minds understand the inner and outer realities freely and without distortion and are capable of coping with a wide range of thoughts, emotions and experiences. Mindfulness means being in the moment with everything that is now, without judgment and without commenting on what is happening. In fact, the mindful elderly is more capable of understanding and managing and solving everyday problems. Mindfulness can increase deeper awareness of difficult emotions and thoughts and reduce stress and improve health. The results of various studies have shown that mindfulness in lifestyle, mental health, emotions, enjoyment of life and expression of anxiety and stress, psychological distress, quality of life (,) Psychological well-being (irrational.) Other factors that may contribute to anxiety are irrational beliefs. Irrational beliefs are desires and goals that become necessary preferences so that they are transformed into anxiety and confusion if not fulfilled. Irregular beliefs in the elderly are thoughts that are dominated by the individual's psyche and are the determinants of how they are interpreted, interpreted, and understood. Events are the regulators of the quality and quantity of behaviors and emotions, irrational beliefs are untrue and disrupt the balance of the individual and hinder successful success in stimulating events. That leads to stress and anxiety in them and makes life difficult for them. Irrelevant beliefs lead to inappropriate emotions (for example, feeling depressed and inferior because of not achieving their goals). The results of various studies have shown that irrational beliefs play a role in anxiety and social functioning, depression, anger and guilt, emotional instability, social and emotional adjustment, and mental health. The phenomenon of aging can be a health condition for the community, lack of proper planning for early prevention of aging problems will lead to a great challenge for the community. An important area of elderly health is the psychological dimension that requires special attention and prevention Elderly people are anxious due to impaired activity and movement, loss of friends Relatives, diminished physical and physical independence, and chronic illnesses are at greater risk of anxiety, and the most common anxiety is death anxiety. Studies in Iran have shown that men's life expectancy is not low for women, since on the other hand, there is a significant relationship between life expectancy and death anxiety.

It is also inferred from existing texts that irrational beliefs and mindfulness are important factors in mental health. Studying the relationship between these variables and important areas of health in the elderly seems necessary. Due to the importance of the topic and contents, the present study aimed to determine the relationship between mindfulness and irrational beliefs with anxiety of elderly and also predicting their death anxiety based on mindfulness and irrational beliefs.

Elderly Definition

Elderly refers to a person over the age of 66 years, who is either at the beginning of his or her retirement or is in the final years of employment. The statistics on the country's elderly population are somewhat confusing, but in recent years the number of elderlies has increased with increasing quality of life, increased health and access to treatment, with the hope of increasing the number of elderlies in the next 15 to 26 years. Increase to nine million. Increasing this age group in our country, in addition to promising to improve living conditions, requires attention by health and safety officials. Elderly, although full of experience, reason, and knowledge, is unfortunately associated with poor physical ability and impaired physical ability, so the elderly also has a number of illnesses after a hard and painful life.

In addition, increasing age increases the likelihood of chronic diseases and older people are more vulnerable to diseases such as cardiovascular disease, diabetes and Alzheimer's disease.

Features of aging

Elderly has several physical, social and psychological characteristics:

1. One of these features is the relative decrease in physical strength that decreases with age as one's physical strengths increase.

2. Another feature of retirement is moving away from past job positions, which leads to a reduction in job-related responsibilities and, as a result, a decrease in one's social connections.

3. Other features include loneliness or loneliness. Especially in cases where one witnesses the loss of one's friends,

relatives, peers, and peers, so he or she becomes more and more lonely every day.

However, it is important that the elderly accept the condition. This acceptance varies among individuals from different cultures, some withholding participation in social life and, in turn, society dismisses them, which deepens the sense of hopelessness and depression in the elderly. But some of the older people with new roles that suit their situation make this course a relatively active and satisfying one.

However, in addition to demographic characteristics, social conditions, and especially the family circumstances of the elderly, are also important. Appropriate family and community conditions can lead a person to accept a new situation and inappropriate family and community conditions can isolate him or her alone. In addition, the level of physical health of the elderly at this stage of life is an important factor in their social life, as for any social participation in the elderly, their health status is first of all considered. Physical wellbeing can help improve social relationships and prevent the onset of depression, but unfortunately increasing age and reaching old age provides the basis for many physical and mental illnesses, including:

Elderly feelings

Feeling of sadness over the neglect of children and their loved ones who have worked for their well-being are the most serious threats to the elderly and are directly linked to their isolation from their surroundings. A man or woman who once considered himself or herself powerful and influential finds himself alone without power, and this discomfort can sometimes lead to inappropriate events and cause elderly psychological distress. Loneliness or loneliness can have profound effects, even affecting the amount of food and metabolism eaten and biological changes. The elderly lack re-sources of friendship because most of them do not work and do not have the opportunity to create friendly relationships in the workplace and have lost some of their age-old friends. This increases their loneliness. These debilitating feelings increase the amount of sedatives and analgesics used in the elderly. Loneliness can cause the elderly to have mental problems, so understanding the elderly feelings and expectations of relatives and correcting family relationships with them is very important in their mental health process. Elderly people do not feel weak and unable to see others as old and disabled. In a warm, kind family, most seniors are comfortable, calm, resilient, and joyful, and even have the patience of grandchildren with all their mischief.

Elderly, due to retirement and away from their children, feel the need for more emotional communication and attention, which needs to be addressed and responded to. Proper planning and use of the elderly and their experiences both eliminate them by themselves and eliminate the feeling of being absent and provide a valuable and valuable source of knowledge and experiences for the next generation of young people.

Elderly people do not have extensive needs, but only hope that their children and relatives will be grateful for their suffering and suffering. Elderly people need love and respect. They would like their children and grandchildren to be consulted and respected as an experienced family member. Satisfying these needs of children and offspring not only costs money but also increases the feeling of goodness within the individual. Remember that the elderly and the elderly, the grandfathers and grandmothers are our roots, we have boiled their fountains and drank their endless seals, and now it is time to support these endless seals and to live the whole experience of life. Let them descend on bowing.

Psychological Changes in Elderly

Given some of the parameters of life, people are living longer than ever before, and the chance or expectation of life is increasing, and consequently we are seeing an increase in the number of older people. To this end, psychological, medical, and rehabilitation services should be provided to adults as much as possible, and mental and physical health professionals should be more attuned to the emotional, mental and physical needs of aging. The older person focuses more on issues, develops hyper-chondriach and delusions, especially about the workings of the cardiovascular system, feels lonely, loses interest in his career and falls into a disadvantageous circle that has the same effects. Suicide in the elderly, which is often taken by surprise and in dangerous ways, is due to depression in 0.080 cases, in others due to minor illnesses, economic problems, loneliness, and so on. Psychomotor activity in the elderly decreases gradually with age. The slowdown in cognitive and motor processes associated with aging is considered the most obvious phenomenon in the field of elderly psychology. Unless there is another obvious pathology due to mental-organ disorders, other cognitive functions in the elderly show slight changes. Elderly people have certain emotional and psychological problems, such as loneliness and inability to attract attention and ownership. If the elderly cannot normally attract the attention and affection of those around them, they resort to behaviors such as conflict. Elderly people may want to control the environment and make others obey themselves to express themselves and relieve stress. Therefore, the locals must first understand the behaviors of the elderly and then try to solve the problems by developing an understanding and good relationship with them. There are significant differences in the treatment of these changes in the elderly. Some of these encounters are briefly mentioned:

- Some seniors deal with changes due to the aging process in a constructive way. This group of elderly people who enjoy their relationships, are well adjusted, and happily accept the old age.
- Some others are dependent and play a passive role. Thinking only of themselves and dealing with new situations. They are scared and out of touch.
- Another group takes on a defensive position. They deal with problems in a rigid and inflexible manner. They strive to

maintain an active life as a young person, always staying away from old age.

- Some seniors deal with the aging process with aggression. This violence may show to family and friends and cause interpersonal problems.
- Others feel self-critical and self-critical and are dissatisfied with themselves. this

The elderly is dissatisfied with their marital life and are not satisfied with their relationships with relatives and friends.

Changes in the physical and psychological state of the elderly are closely linked to sociological factors. The status of the elderly in most industrialized and developed countries depends on their value to society and, as a result, has a relatively low status. With large cities being mechanized and nuclear families replaced by large families, some of the problems of industrial societies are also seen in major cities. In the last two decades, sociologists and social psychologists have emphasized the effects of environmental and social factors on mental health. The role of important life events in the formation of mental illnesses and their relapse has been proven. These important life events such as retirement, spouse death, economic limitations in the elderly are more likely to have a direct impact on their mental health. Healthy older people usually maintain their level of social activity to a degree that is only marginally different from previous years. For many, old age is a period of sustained intelligence, emotional and psychological growth. However, in some cases physical illness or the death of friends may prevent social balance from continuing. In addition, when feelings of isolation peak, so does depression. Today, depression is the most common mental health disorder in people over 65 years of age. Feelings of worthlessness, helplessness, and despair are symptoms of depression. Depression is a mismatch response to loss. Which may be dementia in the elderly. In addition to the classic symptoms of depression, such as sleep and appetite disorder, disinterest in the external world, hints of selfishness, and the idea that life is no longer worth living, one may have memory impairment, difficulty concentrating, judging, and irritability. Also show. Overall, it can be said that depression is one of the most common mental health problems in the elderly. And on the other hand, society is deprived of a wealth of experience, knowledge and maturity of the elderly. According to research done, the elderly homeowner and their isolation are not affected by their premature death. Elderly people who are within the family and community and have a special emotional and respectful attitude are happy and joyful. People who are still able to continue their mental activities are almost normal, even after retirement, and can be employed part-time in the same or previous job. This approach is especially important for seniors who are financially impaired.

Analyzing physical strength limits an older person's performance and activities, and a powerful illness can cause a person to lose their spirits and feel helpless. Elderly is very important from a mental health point of view and should be kept in mind that the most common mental illnesses in the elderly are: elderly psychosis, mental disorders caused by vascular disorders, lack of oxygen, and loss of normal brain activity.

Combined with the decline in social relationships, retirement and loss of loved ones and loved ones.

Elderly and family relationship

Elderly fatigue removal season is a lifetime of trying and enjoying the fruits of many years of hard work, however, reducing social relationships, reducing income, creating long and tiring hours of unemployment can leave the elderly feeling overwhelmed. Look at this difficult period, where by analyzing the mental and physical forces and the influx of disturbing and regrettable thoughts, one of the most important factors in endangering the mental health and health of the elderly and ultimately leading to her mental distress such as depression. Be hurting feelings and emotions and hearing the death toll, the psychological and personal remains of Fred If it endangers, according to the most recently taken almost five million population are aged retirees among an overwhelming majority of those people are living in poverty. According to psychologists, the mental health of the elderly has a great impact on the creation of good and bad minutes in old age, and it should be accepted that observing the mental health of the elderly and creating environmental conditions for them, except through careful examination of life events and health conditions. Existing dilemmas are not possible. Attention is drawn to old age, which, at its peak, leads to the onset or exacerbation of depression. Elderly loneliness, unfulfilled expectations, expectations, anxieties and worries about being in a bad situation, crisis, hopelessness, fear of being taken care of by the elderly, and feeling inadequate and inadequate from other stressful issues Is. On the other hand, numerous studies have shown that the learned helplessness in the elderly is much greater due to some physical, mental and sometimes environmental disabilities. Two psychologists, Langer and Rodin, found in a study that older adults living in conditions with little control over them learned to be helpless as laboratory subjects. For this study, Langar and Rodin allowed residents of one floor of the nursing home to make decisions about their lives. For example, from choosing the type of breakfast to taking care of their pots and arranging the furniture of their rooms. They were even told to take care of themselves in many ways and to do many of the things previously done by the responsible staff. But second-class residents were denied the opportunity to make decisions and were under the control and supervision of responsible staff. All affairs, including accommodation, food and leisure activities, resembled that of the first floor, with the second floor having the least control. For example, every elderly person had a pot or table in their room, but the staff would select or move them. The researchers observed significant differences in both groups of older adults within a few weeks. Seniors who had control and responsibility for their actions were happier, more mentally and physically active, spending more time with others, and 93% of them showed social and personal well-being as well as happiness. But second-class seniors showed the least positive change.

This is not to say that elderly people living at home are immune from any physical or psychological problems. Deficiencies in physical ability, cognition, and analysis of emotional and psychological underpinnings in the aging range due to the presence of a system of causative conditions are inevitable. Rather, it means that older people living at home, in order to enjoy positive living conditions and having good quality conditions, are better at "mental disorder scales" than older people living in a senior home and have a high level of resistance to coping with stress variables. They are aging. Many analytical reasons can justify the results of this study.

Adaptation to Elderly

Aging is a fate that befits all human beings of all genders, races and cultures. It is a time of great enjoyment if it is of good quality. "In today's society, the elderly is part of a larger community. With the advancement of science, people have lived longer and must therefore adapt to the complex psycho-psychological and social changes that occur with aging. With aging, one depends on one's ability to continue and maintain appropriate lifestyles, maintain an active lifestyle, and find suitable alternatives to middle-aged activities.

Among the stresses associated with the death of an elderly spouse, loved ones, and close friends Studies in some countries, including Japan, have shown that older people who have religious beliefs have more mental and physical health benefits than those whose beliefs They are less religious or have no religious beliefs at all, and they are more capable of coping with stress, including the death of loved ones.

These people can return to their mental and physical state more quickly before anxiety and stress occur, and their blood pressure will increase even less. In fact, religious rituals for them act as a relaxation method increasing their adaptability.

Practices such as praying and doing charity and going to pilgrimage accelerate the person's relaxing responses and can be very helpful to the elderly by reducing their anxiety and anxiety.

The belief in life after death, especially the belief that the other world can be better than the present one, makes one feel at ease. The fact that people will be able to see their loved ones again in the future and in the future reduces anxiety in the elderly. One of the other strategies suggested to adapt to the death of loved ones is therapeutic work.

Learning a new profession or day job can increase one's adaptability. On the other hand, the older person can fill the retirement vacuum by replacing new age-appropriate activities with those of previous ones. Working in gardening and gardening, writing, crafting and even helping to keep grandchildren alive can help them feel useful. Proper nutrition in adulthood can have a great impact on mental health and has a physical body.

Depression is said to be reduced by proper nutrition. Foods that have low protein and low carbohydrate and fat are also recommended. Eating smaller portions and more meals to adjust blood glucose to an appropriate extent are more likely to be the case with fish, especially in the elderly. "

What do the elderly need?

The needs of the elderly around the world can be divided into three main groups. The first group is health care needs, which include medical and health care for the elderly. The second group is socio-economic needs such as insurance and pensions that neglecting them will disturb the elderly's psychological, psychological and social peace and the third group is psychological needs.

Social support for the elderly

"The problem of the elderly in traditional and modern societies is one of the most important contemporary mental health challenges. Theorists have divided different aspects of social support into five categories:

1. Emotional support that includes the skill of helping others as they exacerbate stress.
2. Social network support that reduces psychological stress by accessing network membership and helping to forget about problems.
3. Protecting self-esteem, which means that others believe the person has special abilities.
4. Supporting a means of accessing financial resources and services when faced with Stressful Psychological Events.

5. Supporting information that includes providing information to understand stressful events.

Although it is important to have access to social support in general, it is much more beneficial to have self-esteem, especially if it comes from outside the family.

The Role of Continuing Education in Elderly Mental Health

If the rejuvenation of society has been sudden and unexpected in the present circumstances, its aging is quite predictable. So, if community managers are not already thinking of the structures, arrangements, and procedures to deal with such a phenomenon, there will no doubt be a wave of problems in this regard, and in the future the needs of this enormous army cannot be met.

The basic needs of the retired and elderly population

The needs of this population can be broadly categorized into four categories:

1. Financial-economic needs: such as adequate pensions that neglecting social-psychological well-being disrupts this class.

2. Health and needs: such as medical care, medicine, doctors and psychologists and nurses specializing in elderly medicine and psychology.

3. Media Needs: Radio, television, cinema, theater and newspapers and magazines whose content and content audiences are predominantly in this category.

4. Mental needs and attention to their mental health. But mental health and attention to mental needs are also important.

While these strata are in good mental health, this will greatly affect their physical health and improve their social relationships, thus preventing the loss of community costs for their treatment, including high costs. Among the things that greatly contribute to the mental health of retirees are their encouragement to pursue higher education and qualifications. Individuals who have not been able to continue their education during employment for any reason (especially from a post-graduate level) can be encouraged to retire during retirement. Community managers can therefore tailor specific programs to increase the capacity of the disciplines. Consider providing a scholarship or quota for them in universities and higher education centers.

For this reason, our teachings place great emphasis on learning from the elderly and the rebellious. In this article, we will try to look at an elderly person with their characteristics, disadvantages, and needs, because you do not want any of us to have an elder in our family and we need information to communicate with her.

Depression in the elderly

A systematic review was conducted to determine the risk factors for depression among the elderly. The prevalence of depressive symptoms in the elderly has been reported in the range of 100 - 6.9%. These changes may be due to different study environments, methods of measurement, and the use of different tools to measure depression in the study sample.

Loneliness and lack of family support for the causes of depression have been reported in the elderly living in the nursing home. In a study that sought to explore older people's personal views on the effects of hospitalization and care in the nursing home on depression, 80% of the elderly believed that loneliness in old age leads to depression. Also, 88% of the sample believed that lack of family support can cause depression in the elderly. Another study of the elderly showed that feeling alone significantly predicts negative social support and this means That increases loneliness when perceived social support decreases. Therefore, loneliness is partly related to depression through social support. Also, results of another study showed that caring for the elderly during illness plays a protective role in their depression. This care, especially when provided by children, had a greater protective role than non-family members, other family members, and even the patient's own spouse. Another study has also reported that high levels of loneliness are associated with more depressive symptoms in the elderly, so reducing the prevalence of depression in patients from extended family to nuclear can be due to better social emotional support that an individual has. In the extended family.

A study of the elderly has shown that inactivity and inactivity are associated with depressive illness, so that this relationship is stronger in older men than in women. Also, a study of elderly people found that regular walking was effective in reducing their depressive symptoms. In a study comparing the effects of exercise therapy and diet with the approach of weight loss on the level of depression in elderly women with severe depression, Interestingly, this one-year intervention showed that both experimental groups (exercise and diet) There was a greater decrease in the level of depression than the control group. In addition, the physical activity group had a greater improvement in depression than the diet group. In this regard, the study showed that recreational physical activity improved the rate of depression in older women compared to regular physical activity. Physical activity plays a role in reducing the incidence of depression by reducing stress and optimizing brain mechanisms.

A sample of patients admitted to Malaysian hospitals was studied; the results showed that the limiting diseases of the elderly and their dissatisfaction with their personal income were associated with depression, and several studies supported this finding. Low-income people had more depressive symptoms. Other studies also support the link between medical illnesses, forms of daily activities, and depression. The most disabilities were in the areas of mobility, home and family duties, and social participation.

In a study aimed at examining the impact of culture on depression in Chinese immigrant elderly, it was found that those who understood more cultural barriers and identified higher levels of Chinese cultural values had higher levels of depressive symptoms. A study of the role of religion, however, showed that older people's reports of having religion and attending religious services were associated with a lower prevalence of depressive symptoms. In line with this, the results of various studies show that religion and spirituality are associated with less prevalence of depression, better quality of life and even more survival.

The study aimed to determine the social and demographic factors associated with depression in the elderly, in the study group, as predictors of age, sex, place of residence, marital status, educational level, occupation, family type, economic dependency and living conditions. Main Causes of Elderly Depression Introduced Various studies confirm these findings. So that women are more likely to develop depression than married men, single, separated, and widows than married people, those living in nuclear families, illiteracy, living alone, having no children, and unemployment. Grover et al. Showed that depression is more common in women and people with inappropriate economic backgrounds. Based on findings, loneliness and people's perceptions of public health are strong predictors of depression. Various studies have shown that chronic diseases have a significant effect on depression in the elderly, and in addition the metabolic syndrome in the elderly is directly related to the incidence of depression in them. In a study targeting Japanese elderly, individuals were identified. Elderly people who did not consider themselves healthy were more likely to be depressed. On the other hand, numerous studies (both community and clinical) showed heart disease, stroke, arthritis, back pain, diabetes, cancer, and diseases. The kidneys increase the likelihood of depression The Korean elderly showed that health status determined levels of depression. In a study that examined the incidence of metabolic syndrome in depressed patients, 25% of patients with depression had metabolic syndrome criteria. There was also a relationship between metabolic parameters and depression in a group of patients with metabolic syndrome. In another study of outpatients with depression, the prevalence of metabolic syndrome in depressed patients was 36%. This syndrome was associated with the diagnosis of major depression and overeating. On the other hand, some studies found no association between metabolic syndrome and depression. Therefore, a comprehensive study is needed to determine a precise relationship.

According to another study, there was a significant and inverse association between the elderly depression scale and micronutrient assessment scores. Depression in males was inversely associated with poor nutritional status. In addition, there was a significant correlation between Elderly depression scores and red blood cell count, hemoglobin levels or hematocrit values for men. However, the boundary relationship between the depression scale

Elderly and mean erythrocyte volume were observed in women. The findings showed that depression was directly associated with anemia in men. The findings of the study in the elderly show that the duration of mourning and relationship with the deceased, especially when the deceased spouse or child is a predictor of grief in the elderly. On the other hand, grief is one of the factors. Which predicts depression in the elderly. Mourning is also a phenomenon that many older people experience after losing a close relative or a loved one. Therefore, these findings highlight the need for prevention, diagnosis and treatment of elderly people.

From these studies, it is concluded that loneliness and lack of family support, especially in the elderly living in the nursing home, is the most important factor for depression in the elderly because when perceived social support decreases, it increases feelings of loneliness while subject to In chronic diseases, it plays a protective role in the development of depression. Due to the heterogeneity of most studies, it is difficult to compare factors.

Lonely in the elderly

The concept of loneliness is nowadays one of the fundamental issues that have occupied the minds of psychologists, psychotherapists, philosophers, sociologists, and religious thinkers, each explaining this feeling and phenomenon from a different perspective. Although the history of study of loneliness cannot be definitively focused on a specific time frame, in general the study of philosophical schools shows that this concept was emphasized when the human rescuers, including modern reason, were in doubt. The rise of modernity has influenced, more than any other philosophical period, the sense of loneliness in the modern age. Being one of the humanist philosophical schools in response to these concerns of the modern era, it emerged and was quickly adopted, and this school of thought played a central role in explaining human sense of loneliness and its causes. From the perspective of therapists, the phenomenon of loneliness can be studied at three levels of interpersonal, interpersonal, and existential loneliness. Feelings of loneliness can be studied in all ages, but older people, as a large part of society, need further study because of the psychological characteristics of this period.

Given that older age groups are particularly vulnerable due to the negative effects of the aging process and the increased prevalence of loneliness, so assessing loneliness among older people and the problems associated with this phenomenon is an important area of knowledge development and the possibility of intervention. is. The passing of life and reaching old age is potentially unavoidable for all humans. This process is very important to the human person, because neglecting it can cause some disabling problems that, if anticipated in time, and the percentage of preparations needed to cope with them, will greatly exacerbate future problems. We will decrease. Problems and diseases caused by the phenomenon of aging, both in terms of natural aging and diseases of old age, will be of particular importance to people who have some degree of disability or disability. In the hierarchy of natural life, aging is the last stage of life in which one deals with the past. Aging is a process of gradual transformation and understanding of life that is gradually gained through experience. Aging is an accumulation of compensations and substitutes, and the lessons learned by the elders explain many of the traits and lines of their lives. Many elderly people describe aging as a lonely age and fear it as an unpleasant experience. Aging is one of the most critical and decisive stages of human development, which, contrary to popular belief, is not only the end of life, but also as a natural process of passing life. Elderly is a critical period of life and attention to the issues and needs of this stage is a social necessity and attention to health promoting behaviors and quality of life is an important issue that has been neglected. In recent years, attention to the elderly has increased rapidly in countries, especially considering their physical and mental needs, and feeling lonely in all age groups, but is more prevalent in old age.

Feelings of loneliness have been reported as a common problem and negative experiences for older people in scientific societies and health research. Evidence suggests that loneliness is widespread and affects 25-50% of the total population over 65 years of age and sex, and the elderly are at higher risk of feeling lonely. Elderly people are at risk of isolation and loneliness due to reduced interactions due to impaired physical health and death of loved ones. Loneliness is a complex set of feelings and cognitions, distresses, and experiences of negative emotions that arise from perceived individual deficiencies in private and social relationships. Loneliness is a cognitive factor in health and well-being and has serious immediate and long-term consequences on mental health. If the elderly is not lonely, they will have better physical and mental performance. Loneliness is characterized by one's cognitive awareness of weaknesses in one's personal and social relationships that lead to feelings of sadness, emptiness, and regret. In fact, loneliness is the inability to maintain and maintain satisfying relationships with others, which may result in a sense of deprivation. Many qualitative and quantitative studies show that elderly people living with family are healthier than older people living in a nursing home because having a family is accompanied by an emotional and supportive umbrella on the one hand, and on the other. Provides effective and effective social relationships for the elderly with family members, friends and acquaintances, which is very useful and effective in maintaining the mental health of older people. Child migration has a significant effect on elderly parents' sense of loneliness, and this effect persists even with control over other variables. Other variables including general health status, marital status, financial status, and sex of the elderly also had a significant effect on the feeling of loneliness in rural areas. Study. These variables together account for about half of the respondents' sense of loneliness. The results of the study showed that existential therapy reduced the feeling of loneliness and anxiety in the experimental group. Consequently, it is necessary to apply treatments that focus on the elderly 's emotional and emotional problems, in particular the reduction of loneliness and death anxiety. Other research has shown that meaning therapy reduces loneliness in the elderly. One study concluded that loneliness is prevalent in the elderly and associated with negative health consequences for physical and mental health, and adopting appropriate intervention strategies using Ericsson's psychosocial development theory reduces loneliness and improves the quality of life of the elderly and the sense of value in this course is high. There is a significant difference between the elderly living in the nursing home and the elderly living in the families in terms of loneliness, mental health and self-efficacy, as well as living with other family members has a positive impact on the physical and mental health of the elderly, thus considering the socio-cultural status of the elderly. In Iran, the best place to meet their psychological needs is family. The impact of feeling lonely on life satisfaction in the elderly is therefore evident through constant contact with the elderly and identifying unique situations such as diminishing social relationships and identifying the elderly's mentality and beliefs and increasing the awareness of health care providers and families and the elderly about their perceptions. And strengthening relationships and interactions with older people and designing educational, therapeutic, and rehabilitation programs will prevent the feeling of loneliness and life satisfaction in the elderly. Elderly married and satisfied with their life experience less loneliness and also according to the findings of the study elderly who had good general health level were less lonely and feeling lonely is an important factor in reducing general health of the elderly. Since the diagnosis of loneliness can be effective in maintaining the health of the elderly, it is therefore essential that health care team members be aware of the consequences and consequences of loneliness and its effects on health. Music therapy can be used as a strategy to reduce the severity of depression in the elderly; the effect of such interventions can be different between the sexes; and this difference can also be seen in the reduction of loneliness. Elderly view of the phenomenon of feeling lonely is the result of these three themes: feelings of suffering, loss and deprivation and ways of compensation. These subjects provided a vivid picture of the perspective of seniors who had all experienced the phenomenon of loneliness. Elderly experiences of this phenomenon show that they feel loneliness is a painful and painful feeling that results from the lack of life and they communicate with God by reminiscing about different life memories and making new connections to face This phenomenon is trying.

. These findings unveil important concepts in the field of care provision for the elderly and can enhance the ability of health care providers to evaluate, prevent and care for this phenomenon. The limitations of older people's activities, such as walking and engaging in activities, describe interest in problems associated with their loneliness. Negative accidents that conflict with well-being in the elderly can lead to feelings of inadequacy and low self-esteem, and factors that support, such as financial resources or family support, can act to maintain well-being. There is a significant difference in the level of loneliness in the Korean and Japanese elderly home. Korean seniors felt more alone, and most Korean seniors experienced moderate loneliness, and most

Japanese seniors experienced mild loneliness. One of the reasons is the authors of the Korean negative attitude towards living in the elderly home, while the Japanese people have a positive attitude towards this and have a better home life in the elderly home. The Korean elderly also had more depressive symptoms than their Japanese counterparts. The feeling of loneliness among the elderly living in a nursing home is greater than that of the elderly living with their family members. Seniors who had less interaction and were not employed were more likely to feel lonely, and those who had more social support felt less lonely. Interacting with friends and to a lesser extent with neighbors reduces the feeling of loneliness and enhances morale. The feeling of loneliness is associated with being a widow, especially for those who have just lost their spouse. Seniors living with their spouse and family also experience less loneliness than those who live alone or with others other than their spouse. One of the most important causes of loneliness in this study was spouse death and it was much lower in married people than in other groups. A review of research shows that the phenomenon of loneliness is one of the major problems of old age. This feeling of loneliness seems to take over our society more and more in the future due to the growing conditions of our society, such as a tendency not to adopt a child, a tendency to think less about a better life, a generalization to cyberspace and social networks.

Disability in self-care:

Disability in self-care such as wearing clothes, eating, bathing, etc.

makes the elderly feel more alone. In self-care, the elderly tries to live as independently as possible and listen to their inner voice. As seniors age and their disabilities and limitations increase, they are more concerned about losing their self-care ability. In a way, they use all their efforts to maintain their ability to care for and escape this lack of "worst pain" and "scratching". This ability can be so important to Iranian seniors that they prefer death over life without the ability to self-care.

Physical conditions

Other than age, another criterion can help define aging; it is physical and biological transformation. Exceptionally, however, physical aging progresses gradually, so that the moment to be physically old is often contractual. Most people feel that their body strength is depleted between the ages of 30 and 35, but they do not pay much attention to it until their daily activities are affected. Physical aging alters our perception of ourselves, physical aging alerts others that they must change their behavior towards us. Jean-Paul Sartre writes: An old man never feels old. I find out through others that I'm old, but I don't feel old myself

One of the most overlooked problems of suffering is the issue of feeling lonely in the elderly, which many elderly people experience in their communities. Studying the phenomenon of feeling lonely and overcoming it, especially in old age, because of its special nature requires the understanding of different scientific fields such as psychology, psychoanalysis, sociology, especially religion and philosophy. Today it is believed that although it may temporarily alleviate this phenomenon with the help of scientists such as psychology and sociology, the elimination of this undesirable phenomenon is in the shadow of a change in the way people look and know about the origin of the being and how it relates to it. Although philosophical schools' express different reasons for their sense of loneliness in the present man, the causes of loneliness include factors such as inability to take care of themselves, marry and divorce children, and decease their husbands and reduce social relationships. Research findings show that 58 percent of seniors over 65 need help with their daily activities, and the highest quality of life in seniors is seen when they have the support of their spouse, children and friends. Elderly caregivers may experience stress or irritability due to the particular circumstances of the elderly person's care and may be mistreated by the elderly. Caregivers need to be taken into consideration, too, with the conditions for mental discharge or periods of rest for them being 3.43% of the stress in the family due to a malfunction in family functioning. Lack of sufficient awareness, lack of caring motivation and any cases that are the source of malfunctioning family can lead to abuse. It has been found that there is a high relationship between elder abuse and physical and economic dependence of the elderly, especially when financial burden is placed on caregivers. The findings of a recent study also suggested that older women are more likely to be exposed to abuse because they are economically more dependent on their caregivers. The study found that many behaviors that the elderly and their caregivers consider to be normal behavior are abusive. This is due to the lack of awareness of the elderly and their caregivers. The burden on others has been to lack, be independent, and maximize their ability to influence the preservation of dignity and reduce the sense of loneliness in the elderly. Many people raise their voices when faced with the elderly because they have such a closed mind that the elderly have poor hearing ability and may not be able to hear the sound well. This is true because the elderly suffers from a phenomenon called gingivitis, although the gingival severity is not the same for all seniors and not all so-called seniors are heavy. There was a significant relationship between visual and hearing impairment, disability in movement and activity, and a feeling of perpetual loneliness. Modern science proposes different ways to reduce and overcome this feeling of loneliness. Communication with God and worship are used as a basic way of dealing with feelings of loneliness. Communication with the origin of existence is one of the most basic ways of feeling lonely in individuals. There is a relationship between religious attitudes and factors related to feelings of loneliness, such as well-being and mental health, anxiety and depression. Increasing social skills in the elderly can reduce this feeling of loneliness in the elderly. The role of these skills is to reduce the feeling of loneliness. Seniors who have more children Contrary to popular belief, they have higher expectations of their children than seniors with fewer children. Considering the importance of the role of the family in reducing the sense of loneliness in the elderly, it is necessary to adopt health education programs for elderly families.

Keeping away from familiar home environments and family supports, along with the weaknesses of abilities, skills and abilities of adolescence, can provide the basis for psychological problems for the elderly living in the nursing home; therefore, it is necessary to seek and identify factors that affect the elderly. To alleviate these problems. One of the most effective and neglected factors is hope.

Recommendations for Mental Health

1. Reduce stress (anxiety and worry)

Stress has various effects on physical functions, hypertension, nervous system function, thinking, mood, concentration and memory. The chemicals that the body produces during stress cause negative effects on the brain, thus impairing concentration, learning, and memory function at an early age. For example, staying in traffic during busy hours on the streets can be stressful. So, it can be counteracted by adjusting

commuting times or changing routes. If forced grooming keeps the kids tired and stressed out, they can find a solution to the problem. Things like walking, playing sports and having fun, and using relaxation techniques (meditation and yoga) for a few days off can help reduce stress.

2. Protecting the brain and preventing its damage:

Falling is the most common brain injury in the elderly. These injuries can lead to a decrease in brain capacity, so this valuable organ must be properly protected. In order to avoid falling over the barriers of the elderly and places where walking is likely to slip, they should be corrected and there should always be adequate light in the house. Talk to your GP if you are feeling unbalanced while standing or walking.

3. Maintain social relationships.

Support from social relationships with friends, family, relatives, and co-workers helps maintain mental health. Studies have shown that those with good relationships with family members, relatives, and social groups exhibit Alzheimer's symptoms later than those who are isolated and unrelated, so it is recommended that the elderly maintain these relationships. Voluntary social activities and participation in different groups are helpful.

4. Spiritual communication:

If spiritual or spiritual issues make you feel good, try to keep in touch. Any religious or spiritual beliefs you are trying to reinforce. They may help alleviate depression in the elderly or even be a defense against Alzheimer's. Those who have strong religious and spiritual beliefs usually feel more supportive and comfortable. What things help preserve memory in old age? First of all, don't be afraid to ask and say "you forgot something" and don't be embarrassed. Don't expect to remember everything.

5. Use notes, mark things on the calendar, and anything else that helps with memory.

6. Proper nutrition is needed to maintain memory strength. Consume a little sugar, fat, and salt, but increase the consumption of fresh fruits and vegetables.

7. Keeping an eye on when learning new content improves memory and learning, so try to eliminate additional stimuli in the environment and focus on the subject.

8. Allowing more time for learning facilitates remembering and remembering.

9. Store things you always use, such as glasses or a key, in a designated place, for example, in a large bowl in the living room.

10. Listen to the radio or television news every day. Try to learn something new every day. Read a book or newspaper.

11. In the midst of friends or family, describe past memories. You can look at old photo albums to remember people's names and memories.

12. Leave a notepad next to the phone. Every time someone calls, if they have a message or want something from you, take notes immediately. This will help you not forget the phone messages.

Danger Symptoms

These symptoms are not natural components of aging and may indicate the presence of a disease so it is advisable to consult a physician or counselor.

1. A depressed and sad mood that lasts more than two weeks.

2. Repeated thoughts about death, death, or suicide. Suicidal thoughts require an immediate referral to a physician or psychiatrist.

3. Losing interest and pleasure in things or people who already have a positive feeling.

4. Abnormal fatigue, lethargy and feeling powerless.

5. Irritability, bickering, repeated arguments or aggression.

6. Significant loss or increase in appetite and weight loss.

7. Changing sleep status such as insomnia at the beginning or end of the night or sleeping more than usual.

8. Feeling worthless or feeling guilty, hopeless or feeling inferior.

One of the important areas of elderly health is the mental dimension that requires special attention and prevention of disorders such as anxiety in

It is them. Death anxiety as an abnormal fear of dying undermines effective adaptation. The present study aimed to predict elderly death anxiety was based on mindfulness and irrational beliefs.

Aging is the last stage of life in which the individual undergoes a transitional process. The accumulative broad-based activity is one of compensations and substitutes, and the lessons learned by the pirates explain many of the complexities and lines of their conversion. The series of changes that occur with increasing age especially with approaching old age, such as the death of relatives, the loss of power, the weakness of physical abilities, and the approaching end-of-life stressors, affect specific stressors. And it affects their physical and mental health. Considering that mental health as one of the pillars of health and the necessity of a productive, effective and satisfying life, the promotion of the mental health of individuals in a community requires the dynamism, well-being and excellence of that community. Research has shown that physical and social well-being in which the elderly live affects their social experiences, mental health, well-being and adaptability. The elderly often like to stay in their own home, deeply in their home as a place reminiscent of their past memories, fond of independence, and the love of you and your neighbors and distant neighbors. In addition, social support in family settings plays a powerful role in reducing stress, thereby enhancing physical and mental health. Putting the elderly in nursing homes or care centers can cause a lot of problems. Many early studies have focused on the physical health of these elderly. However, their psychological status is far from being examined. Research has shown that the prevalence of mental disorders in the elderly is increasing, with some calling it a crisis. The rate of these disorders is projected to increase fourfold by four times a year. A study of 1 in 8 elderly people showed that 3 and 4 percent of the elderly had symptoms of mental disorder over the past one and twelve months, respectively. They take it.

Psychological abnormalities in the elderly have many undesirable consequences, and in addition to increasing their physical disability, one of the main causes of suicide among the elderly. It is noted that about 2% of suicide victims in the sample had at least one of the first diagnostic features of the DSM IV-R axis, while that in other populations was 7%. The number of older people in industrialized and developing societies is increasing as life expectancy and fertility decline. Estimates show that the population of the elderly (over 5 years) will exceed 1 billion by year, accounting for 5% of the world's population. On the other hand, advances in medical science and increased competence among diseases are leading to an increase in the prevalence of diseases in the elderly population.

Therefore, trying to identify the psychological disorders of the elderly and to estimate their prevalence and identify the factors that are effective in preventing these problems is one of the first necessary measures to help improve the quality of life of the elderly. In the field of psychological studies of mental health, two approaches can be seen. The first approach focuses more on psychological disorders and related factors, but on the second and newer approaches to positive factors (resilience, religious experiences, wit, efficacy, etc.) affecting prevention it is possible. Hope and hope are one of the positive and influential factors in productive and healthy aging. Some scholars believe that the notion of hopefulness is a concept that is related to compliance, trust, and empowerment, by accepting existing conditions as an effective response to change. Hopefulness reinforces physiological and psychological function, the absence of which leads to premature autopsy in one's functioning. Hope is an intrinsic quality that can energize the individual. For these reasons, hopeful people feel more responsible for their own care, responding well to the efforts of others to take care of them. Several studies have examined the role of hope in mental disorders, especially in the late stages of life. The perspective that people face when they are questioning is death, and they feel that they have to do what they have to do and have no intention of trying. Being with the family and enjoying their respect and attention can maintain a sense of usefulness and efficiency in the elderly, and still maintain a life expectancy, but it seems unlikely that this would be the case for the elderly resident.

Elderly is a stage of human evolution that is accompanied by poor physical abilities, cognitive skills, retirement and loss experience. All of these factors, along with being away from home and family, provide conditions for elderly caregivers that make them more vulnerable to psychological problems and problems. What one should know today is not just prolonging life. Rather, it should seek to ensure that one's years of life are finally spent in peace and physical and mental health. Therefore, estimating the prevalence of mental disorders among the elderly and identifying the factors affecting mental health and resilience to mental disorders should be an essential step in planning and research in the field of aging. The findings of the study showed a high prevalence of mental disorders (1.9%) among the elderly resident. Given the inclusion and exclusion criteria of the study sample, the prevalence of these disorders in the community may be much higher, and the changes in the physical and psychological status of the person concerned may be closely related to environmental and environmental issues. The leading position in most industrialized nations depends on their labor value for social protection, and consequently their relative dignity and dignity. Developing societies like ours need big cities to transform their families and move families from widespread to nuclear in order to experience the complexities of institutionalized societies that reduce social relationships, reduce income, create long-lasting and tiring hours. It may seek refuge in the family law and increase emotional connection with them to reduce it. But the loneliness and the unfulfilled, unfulfilled expectations of those around, entrusted to the elderly, the feeling of being ostracized by the family and the surroundings, the inadequate feeling of being inundated with stressful things. Most of them are caused by psychological problems. There is also much more to be said about the results of some of the studies of helplessness that have been learned in the study due to some physical and some social and environmental disabilities. Elderly residents living in a dry, formal environment can have little control over their condition, and thus become ill. There was a high correlation between some of the psychological variables in the questionnaires such as poor control over life, depression and decreased self-efficacy. Emotional discomfort over elderly caregivers has been reported as another issue. In examining one of the most effective and resistant factors to psychological disorders, hope had a significant relationship with personality traits, namely, those who reported higher levels of hope and anxiety were less likely to report symptoms of depression. Illness and prevention of abnormalities can contribute to mental illness. Hope is defined as a goal-oriented cognitive process and a process of thinking about one's goals, along with the motivation to move toward the goals of operational hope and (methods of achieving goals) strategic hope. The goal setting is the driving force and the willpower of the three main parts of hope. Adult hopefuls must have a certain psychological profile. Adults with high levels of hope have experienced other failures in their lives, but have developed this belief that they can cope with the challenges and cope with the challenges. They continue a positive, positive internal conversation, including statements from the tribe of "I can handle it, I will not give up" and as such. These people experience negative emotions and severe comorbidities when they reach valuable goals, resulting in greater mental health and poorer mental and psychological well-being. Based on the results of Hope Research, it is able to predict the effects of medical interventions, mental health, high quality of life, avoidance of stressful situations, happiness in life, problem solving ability and elderly efficacy. Hope also affects the quality of relationships with others so that desperate people can rarely be elated with other pleasantries, and then always feel lonely and hopeless. Lack of hope or motivation for prolonged confrontation with physical and life-threatening events or inevitable events in life can have serious effects on one's psyche and body. Hope is one of the human traits that helps him to overcome disappointments, pursue his goals, and reduce the feeling of unbearable future. Hopeful people are healthier and happier, their immune systems work better, and get away with better mental stress by utilizing effective coping strategies such as reassessment and problem solving. Given the high prevalence of psychiatric disorders in the elderly resident in the elderly, attention to the psychological status of this group should be at the top of the work priorities to identify effective factors and to take effective measures to identify them.

Relationships between mindfulness and irrational beliefs with elderly death anxiety Relationships are highly correlated. There was a significant relationship between mindfulness and death anxiety. The elderly who reported high consciousness had low death anxiety. In contrast, the elderly with low consciousness had high anxiety of death. Living in a conscious mind makes seniors more aware of themselves, their abilities, and their surroundings, and thus more hopeful and optimistic in life. The mentally retarded elderly loses the ability to be realistic, consider many of the weaknesses and dark aspects of life, and suffer from unpleasant emotions such as depression and anxiety. Elderly people with a high level of consciousness are more aware of their daily activities and are more familiar with the automatic features of their mind (such as the tendency to flee from the present and into the past and the future) and gain moment-to-moment awareness in They cultivate themselves. Mindfulness can be viewed as opposed to situations such as mental occupation with memories, imaginations, plans, or concerns and the automatic behavior of the elderly, where attention is focused on something else. Mindfulness causes awareness to increase emotions and reduce stress. Accordingly, seniors with high levels of consciousness are less likely to experience stress and less likely to suffer death anxiety. Also, seniors with high levels of consciousness will enjoy a better lifestyle and mental health. Mindfulness is one of the influencing factors in anxiety, stress and psychological distress. On the other hand, people with a high level of consciousness will enjoy their life more and will enjoy high psychological well-being and quality of life. Overall, it can be concluded that mindfulness is one of the influencing factors in elderly death anxiety.

There was a significant relationship between irrational beliefs and death anxiety. In explaining the result, all kinds of irrational beliefs are the root cause of human problems. Events and events around people do not cause them stress or anxiety, but the views and beliefs of people about events and events that lead to stress and anxiety in their lives. The root of many human behavioral and mental disorders is rooted in irrational beliefs about the world around us. Long-term irrational beliefs can cause anxiety and lead to mental disorders. Beliefs are basically divided into logical and irrational categories. Logical beliefs are efficient beliefs that help one achieve their important, realistic, logical, and flexible goals. In contrast, irrational beliefs are ineffective beliefs that prevent one from attaining their personal goals and having unrealistic characteristics. Unreasonable beliefs reduce social functioning and are one of the factors influencing anxiety. Elderly people with irrational beliefs are more likely to feel guilty and angry and to have higher anxiety of death. Such seniors are more likely to be depressed and will report high emotional instability. On the other hand, irrational beliefs are influential factors in social adjustment. Unreasonable beliefs dominate the psyche and are the determinants of how one interprets and interprets events and regulates the quality and quantity of behaviors and emotions. Unreasonable beliefs affect mental health and lead to depression, self-blame, remorse, and other profound emotional effects. Marital status was one of the demographic factors that influenced elderly death anxiety. In addition, income status was another demographic factor that significantly predicted the anxiety of elderly death. Seniors living with their spouse and having a good income are more likely to have higher spiritual health than other seniors and will report less death anxiety.

conclusion

Hypertension is high among nursing home residents; hope as one of the most important human cognitive traits with a better expectation for the future can play a very effective role in preventing mental illness in the elderly living at home. Therefore, it is necessary to work in various ways to hopefully maintain and improve the morale of the elderly and thus help to maintain their mental health and improve their quality of life.

REFERENCES

Lunenfeld B. The ageing male: demographics and challenges. World journal of urology. 2002;20(1):11-6.

Kok R. Atypical presentation of depression in the elderly: fact or fction?. Tijdschrift voor gerontologie en geriatrie. 2004;35(2):65-71.

Mueller TI, Kohn R, Leventhal N, Leon AC, Solomon D, Coryell W, et al. The course of depression in elderly patients. The American journal of geriatric psychiatry. 2004;12(1):22-9.

R K. Depression in the elderly. Depression in the elderly Division of Geriatric Medicine, St Louis School of Medicine. 2005.

Lai DW. Impact of culture on depressive symptoms of elderly Chinese immigrants. Canadian Journal of Psychiatry. 2004;49(12):820-7.

Bruce ML. Psychosocial risk factors for depressive disorders in late life.

Biological psychiatry. 2002;52(3):175-84.

Cole MG, Dendukuri N. Risk factors for depression among elderly community subjects: a systematic review and meta-analysis. American Journal of Psychiatry. 2003.

Blazer D. Depression in the elderly. New England Journal of Medicine. 1989;320(3):164-6.

Chang-Quan H, Xue-Mei Z, Bi-Rong D, Zhen-Chan L, Ji-Rong Y, Qing-Xiu L. Health status and risk for depression among the elderly: a meta-analysis of published literature. Age and Ageing. 2010;39(1):23-30.

Von Korff M, Ormel J, Katon W, Lin EH. Disability and depression among high utilizers of health care: a longitudinal analysis. Archives of general psychiatry. 1992;49(2):91.

Wells KB, Burnam MA. Caring for depression in America: lessons learned from early fndings of the medical outcomes study. Psychiatric medicine. 1990;9(4):503-19.

Press Y, Tandeter H, Romem P, Hazzan R, Farkash M. Depressive symptomatology as a risk factor for increased health service utilization among elderly patients in primary care. Archives of gerontology and geriatrics. 2012;54(1):127-30.

Huang H, Menezes PR, da Silva SA, Tabb K, Barkil-Oteo A, Scazufca M. The association between depressive disorders and health care utilization: Results from the Sao Paulo Ageing and Health study (SPAH). General hospital psychiatry. 2014;36(2):199-202.

Bock J-O, Luppa M, Brettschneider C, Riedel-Heller S, Bickel H, Fuchs A, et al. Impact of Depression on Health Care Utilization and Costs among

Multimorbid Patients–Results from the MultiCare Cohort Study. PloS one. 2014;9(3):e91973.

Van Alphen S, Rossi G, Segal D, Rosowsky E. Issues regarding the proposed DSM-5 personality disorders in geriatric psychology and psychiatry. International Psychogeriatrics. 2013;25(01):1-5.

Runcan PL. Elderly institutionalization and depression. Procedia-Social and Behavioral Sciences. 2012;33:109-13.

Ciucurel C, Iconaru EI. The importance of sedentarism in the development of depression in elderly people. Procedia-Social and Behavioral Sciences. 2012;33:722-6.

Pandit D, Manna N, Datta M, Biswas S, Baur B, Mundle M. Depression and associated socio-demographic factors among Geriatrics-An Experience from a tertiary Hospital. IOSR Journal of Dental and Medical Sciences. 2013;8(5):35-8.

Kim O, Byeon Y-S, Kim J-H, Endo E, Akahoshi M, Ogasawara H. Loneliness, depression and health status of the institutionalized elderly in Korea and Japan. Asian nursing research. 2009;3(2):63-70.

Yaka E, Keskinoglu P, Ucku R, Yener GG, Tunca Z. Prevalence and risk factors of depression among community dwelling elderly. Archives of gerontology and geriatrics. 2014;59(1):150-4.

Ciucurel C, Iconaru EI. Association between metabolic syndrome and depression in elderly. Procedia-Social and Behavioral Sciences. 2012;33:994-7.

Lucchetti G, Lucchetti AL, Peres MF, Moreira-Almeida A, Koenig HG. Religiousness, Health, and Depression in Older Adults from a Brazilian Military Setting. ISRN psychiatry. 2012;2012.

De Rezende CA, Coelho L, Oliveira L, Penha-Silva N. Dependence of the geriatric depression scores on age, nutritional status, and haematologic variables in elderly from a pilot randomized trial. Mental Health and Physical Activity. 2009;2(2):71-5.

Koster A, Bosma H, Kempen GI, Penninx BW, Beekman AT, Deeg DJ, et al. Socioeconomic differences in incident depression in older adults: the role of psychosocial factors, physical health status, and behavioral factors. Journal of psychosomatic research. 2006;61(5):619-27.

Steunenberg B, Beekman AT, Deeg DJ, Kerkhof AJ. Personality and the onset of depression in late life. Journal of affective disorders. 2006;92(2):243-51.

Sawatzky R, Ratner PA, Chiu L. A meta-analysis of the relationship between spirituality and quality of life. Social indicators research. 2005;72(2):153-88.

Grover S, Dutt A, Avasthi A. An overview of Indian research in depression. Indian journal of psychiatry. 2010;52(7):178.

Rauch SA, Morales KH, Zubritsky C, Knott K, Oslin D. Posttraumatic stress, depression, and health among older adults in primary care. The American journal of geriatric psychiatry. 2006;14(4):316-24.

Akechi T, Nakano T, Akizuki N, Okamura M, Sakuma K, Nakanishi T, et al. Somatic symptoms for diagnosing major depression in cancer patients. Psychosomatics. 2003;44(3):244-8.

Patten SB. Long-term medical conditions and major depression in the Canadian population. Canadian Journal of Psychiatry. 1999;44:151-7.

Richter N, Juckel G, Assion H-J. Metabolic syndrome: a follow-up study of acute depressive inpatients. European archives of psychiatry and clinical neuroscience. 2010;260(1):41-9.

Heiskanen TH, Niskanen LK, Hintikka JJ, Koivumaa-Honkanen HT,

Honkalampi KM, Haatainen KM, et al. Metabolic syndrome and depression: a cross-sectional analysis. The Journal of clinical psychiatry. 2006;67(9):1,478-1427.

Diaz-Martinez L, Serrano N, Pinzon J, Mantilla G, Velasco H, Martinez L, et al. [Lack of association between metabolic syndrome and depressive symptoms in Colombian adults]. Revista medica de Chile. 2007;135(8):990-6.

Muhtz C, Zyriax B-C, Klähn T, Windler E, Otte C. Depressive symptoms and metabolic risk: effects of cortisol and gender. Psycho neuroendocrinology. 2009;34(7):1004-11.

Koenig HG. Religion and depression in older medical inpatients. The American journal of geriatric psychiatry. 2007;15(4):282-91.

Shah SN, Meeks S. Late-life bereavement and complicated grief: A proposed comprehensive framework. Aging & mental health. 2012;16(1):39-56.

www.ingramcontent.com/pod-product-compliance
Lightning Source LLC
Chambersburg PA
CBHW071752040426
42446CB00012B/2526